A Guide to Nursery Pre-school Educatio

GETTING A GOOD START

One minute they are crying and dribbling, the next minute we are looking for an institution for them to attend. The speed with which young children move from being babies to starting pre-school education is absolutely astonishing. But then, almost everything about the early years of children's lives is amazing. At the age of two they are speaking odd words, by three they talk in sentences, and at the age of four most children, in whatever country they live – Britain, Russia, Brazil, China – have a vocabulary of thousands of words and a grasp of 90 per cent of the grammar and syntax of their native language.

The first five years of a child's life are a phase of rapid growth, development and learning. The initial helplessness and dependency of babyhood does not last long and, by the time they are ready for school, most children will have reached amazing levels of competence, not just in their mastery of language, but in control of their own body and in their ability to make decisions and think for themselves. Because this phase of development is so rapid, children have enormous potential for learning.

Parents are a child's first teachers, and have the daunting but exciting task of making sure that the best possible start is made on a lifelong journey of learning. Whether a child has one or two parents, what matters is the *quality* of parenting, because children's early experiences have a lasting influence on their success in school and in later life.

Although parents are the first, and most important educators of their children, other people will have a significant role to play in the first five years. Most children will experience different forms of care and education outside their own home, as they visit relatives and friends, and responsibility for child-rearing becomes a shared process. All these people can be called 'caregivers', because that is what they do. So choosing any form of childcare, or a setting outside the home, whether this is a nursery, playgroup or something else, is a decision which requires careful thought and planning.

There are many good reasons for children to attend some form of provision before they start school. Here are just five:

1. encouraging children to socialize with their peers and other adults;
2. extending their opportunities for learning in different situations;
3. preparing them for school;
4. giving parents a break;
5. giving parents and caregivers opportunities to meet together, share interests and develop networks of people who can support each other.

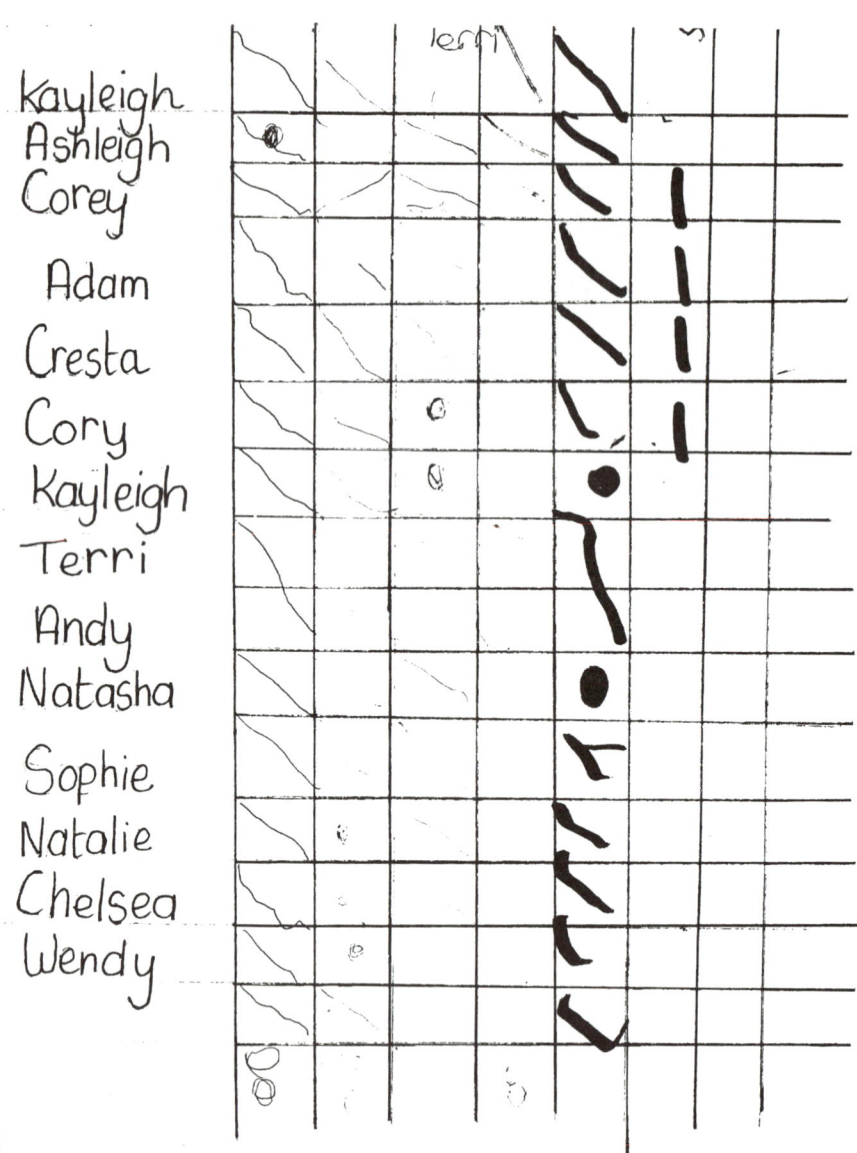

Every morning, Terri filled in the register before her Mum left the nursery. She liked to role play being the teacher, 'counted' how many of her friends had arrived and wrote the numbers at the bottom

WHAT CHOICES ARE THERE?

- Alice and Jim Harper live on a small farm. Jim works long hours and Alice helps when she can. They would like Jason, their two year old, to be able to play with other children. Perhaps a playgroup is the answer.

- Jane Sherwood is a single parent with three children. The two oldest go to the local primary school but Gemma, her three year old, gets bored at home on her own. Maybe a place in a nursery school is needed.

- Poonam Mehta has two children, Asha and Umesh, aged one and three. Her husband works, and she has the chance to go back to the well-paid job she used to have. Perhaps they can afford a nanny to look after the two children during the day.

WHAT CHOICES ARE THERE? 3

Giving parents a break

- Eddie Sewell is a single parent, bringing up three-year-old Samantha on his own. He does not have a job, but he could get part-time work if someone would look after Samantha when the jobs come up. Maybe a registered childminder could help.

The needs of families can differ widely. Some parents may need full-time provision for their children throughout the first five years to fit in with their employment. Other parents may want to dip into different settings, such as parent and toddler groups, playgroups and, where available, a nursery class, or even an early start at school.

It is generally accepted that attending some form of provision outside the home can be beneficial to children as it helps them to become social and sociable. For example, they will learn to share, to wait their turn and to help each other, all very useful for when they start school. They will extend the whole range of their experience with other grown-ups and children. So let us look at the choices available to parents and children, and see how we can maintain the quality of experience which is essential for this age group.

Provision and services for children under five and their families vary widely between areas, so what you might want may not actually be available. Local authorities have had little extra money to spend on education, so much of the recent expansion in provision has come from the private sector.

Many parents either decide or have to return to work as soon as their period of maternity or paternity leave is over. Choosing a suitable form of childcare can be a difficult process. The choices made will depend on how much you are able and willing to pay, the type of childcare preferred and the demands of the working day. Some parents may have little or no cash available and be looking for a free nursery place, others might be able to afford to pay an individual, or buy a place in a centre somewhere.

There are two basic options – *home-based* (like childminders and nannies) and *centre-based* (like nurseries and playgroups), both of which should provide not only care but also education.

HOME-BASED PROVISION

Childminders

Childminders are allowed to provide home-based childcare for a certain number of children, depending on the age of the children. They offer flexible hours according to individual needs, and parents pay accordingly. Many now provide a service during school holidays to meet the needs of working parents. However, if they are not required at such times, often a small retainer is charged.

The Children Act (1989) states that childminders who look after a child for more than two hours per day have to be registered with the local authority and be inspected to ensure that provision is in line with certain standards. The inspection process looks at safety, the environment, facilities and the quality of education offered. The local authority keeps a list of registered childminders, and those who fail to meet the standards are deregistered. This is primarily to ensure that children receive good quality care and education in a fast-growing sector of preschool provision.

Entering into an arrangement with a childminder is not simply a case of agreeing fees and hours. Parents are entrusting the care of a child to another adult who will become a principal caregiver. It is important to establish some shared values and common approaches to preserve continuity and stability for the child. Parents will also want to communicate on a daily basis about the child's experiences, health and significant milestones in development. Childminders who have undergone some training for this important role will ensure that they establish good relationships with their clients, because they have a shared interest in the child's well-being and know they provide a vital service.

Nannies

These are not just people who look after royalty nowadays. Most do not go round looking like Mary Poppins. Nor, fortunately, do they levitate and fly through the air. Some parents who go out to work like to employ somebody to look after their children in their own homes. Often nannies will take on some housekeeping responsibilities as well, but reasonable expectations have to be negotiated at the outset. Many nannies are trained 'nursery nurses' who have taken a two-year specialist course in all aspects of childcare, early learning and development. Although training is not compulsory, and anyone can call themselves a nanny, it is advisable to have somebody who is reliable, trustworthy and who will provide the right kinds of activities and stimulation that a young child needs.

If children have either a childminder or a nanny, some parents may also want them to have some form of centre-based provision to meet and play with other children, so this should be negotiated as part of the arrangements.

CENTRE-BASED PROVISION

There are many types of centre-based daycare for young children in both the private and public sectors, including nurseries and playgroups. All forms of provision are inspected by the local authority and have to comply with standards set by the

Children Act (1989) on health, safety, the training and qualifications of staff, appropriate educational activities and good quality provision for play. There are precise ratios for the number of adults to children. This varies according to the age of the children in each group, but it must be maintained at all times.

PUBLIC SECTOR PROVISION

For parents without any form of financial help from an employer, private childcare can be expensive. However, if you are on a low income, you may be able to obtain a place at a *local authority day nursery* or *combined centre*. The fees charged are usually based on your ability to pay, and both often provide a range of family support services.

Day nurseries

These are run by the social services department and provide full-time or part-time places. Usually they are staffed by nursery nurses and care assistants, and the officers in charge are required to have a qualification in childcare, education, social work, health visiting or children's nursing. Children who are identified as being 'in need' or 'at risk' are often given priority in day nurseries, and staff can liaise with a range of specialists in child health and education to support them and their families. The emphasis is on liaison with parents, so that shared approaches can be maintained for the benefit of the child.

Combined centres

Run jointly by the education and social services department, these are staffed by adults with qualifications in health, education and social work. As with day nurseries, they combine care, education and family support services. The centres offer full- or part-time care with extended hours, and are usually open for 50 weeks of the year. Some provide after-school care for primary age children and a range of services for the community including adult education classes.

Nursery schools and classes

Some public sector provision is specifically for three- and four-year-old children. Although parents are not legally bound to send children to school until they are five years old there is some state-provided *nursery education* in classes attached to primary schools, or in separate nursery schools. Provision is usually part time, but some have a proportion of full-time places, particularly in areas where availability is widespread.

Nursery schools and classes are run by qualified teachers and nursery nurses. This type of provision is very much in demand from parents, as there is traditionally a greater emphasis on education, followed by a smooth transfer into the primary school.

Parents should also check the entry policy at their local primary school. Some now like to start all four year olds or 'rising fives' together in September. Others have maintained two intakes in September and January, and some still have a third intake in April.

PRIVATE SECTOR PROVISION

The private sector offers a number of options including *day nurseries*, *workplace nurseries* and *independent schools*. Day and workplace nurseries usually provide flexible hours according to parents' needs, are open throughout the year and cater for children under five. Independent schools may have a preschool or kindergarten department which opens during school hours, but some may provide care out of school hours for working parents. They usually cater for three to five year olds, exceptionally for two year olds.

Some companies have 'family friendly' policies for their employees, so they provide assistance with fees at workplace nurseries to enable parents with young children to return to work without undue stress. Often this enables you to see your children during the day, and this can provide reassurance for children, easing the difficult transition to sharing responsibility for child-rearing. Some companies provide employees with a childcare subsidy, which can be used according to parents' preferences. For example, some parents prefer to use facilities near home, to avoid long journeys to and from work.

VOLUNTARY SECTOR PROVISION

Unfortunately, provision for children under five is uneven and, in some areas, sparse. The 'voluntary' sector is exactly what it says, a 'self-help' way of getting children together. Playgroups have filled some of the gaps, especially for children in rural areas, where they are often the only form of provision available. Playgroups began in the early 1960s, because parents were frustrated with the lack of nursery places for their children.

This whole self-help movement was originally known as the 'Preschool Playgroups Association'. It has grown substantially, but has maintained its original philosophy of being run by parents. It is now known as the *Preschool Learning Alliance* (PLA) as the focus has shifted to learning through play and preparing children for school. The emphasis is still on parental involvement, and on strengthening the parents' role as the child's first educator. Most playgroups are affiliated to the PLA.

Typically playgroups offer parents a choice of the number of sessions they wish their child to attend. In areas of high demand places may be limited and, if there is nothing else available, parents will usually take what is on offer. Some playgroups make it a priority to give the older children more sessions to help prepare them for school.

Facilities may be limited due to lack of space

Playgroups are funded by a combination of fees, grants and fund-raising. They are run by volunteers, usually parents. Some are even qualified teachers, taking a break to raise their family, others may have taken a PLA training course. Small groups may be run in a parent's home, but usually sessions are held in local centres such as church halls and scout huts. Their strength is that they offer relatively low-cost provision and are responsive to local needs. However, facilities and equipment are sometimes limited because of the lack of space and resources, and there may be restricted opportunities for outdoor play.

There has been a trend towards playgroups being run on school premises. Where this happens there are often significant benefits from contacts with teachers of the youngest classes of five to seven year olds, sharing outdoor play space, and resources. This also helps to provide children with continuity, from playgroup to nursery or reception class.

CLUBS, GROUPS AND CENTRES

In addition to the main forms of provision outlined above there are a range of clubs, voluntary groups, and drop-in centres which provide different facilities.

- *Parent and toddler groups* are run by a variety of organizations and can spring up in all sorts of places in the local community. They are run by volunteers on a self-help basis, and a small fee may be charged for each session. The number and length of sessions is variable, but generally parents and carers meet for a couple of hours and still take responsibility for their children while they are playing.

- *Lunchtime clubs and playcentres* are run by some local authority leisure departments. Again these provide opportunities for parents to meet and for their children to experience different forms of play.

- *Family centres* focus on parents and children. They provide a range of advisory and support services. You can also obtain advice on health, nutrition, state benefits and services for children. Some centres run parentcraft classes and support groups and may provide childcare facilities. They are a useful focal point for the local community and can provide a place to meet other parents and children.

- *Toy and book libraries* are an important resource for parents. Keeping up with young children's appetites for variety and stimulation can be an expensive business. *Toy libraries* operate in mobile vans for rural areas, and some are run by playgroups or nursery schools. They are staffed by trained workers who can give advice about what types of toys and games to select, their educational potential, and how parents can develop their skills as players with their children. Being able to play with and alongside a child can help to support their learning and development.

- *Book libraries* have become much more 'child friendly' in recent years. Back in the distant past some librarians regarded it as a major defeat if any child actually took a book out, or if a page ever got a mark on it. That defensive attitude has changed and it is not unusual to see displays of children's art work, either from home or a local preschool group. As well as stocking a wide variety of books and audiotapes, and also, nowadays, new technology like CD ROMs, which children often love, some have quiet areas where parents and children can choose, or read together. Some libraries have story reading sessions, and librarians are trained to advise on suitable materials for different ages. There is a wide recognition of the importance of 'catching them young' in order to

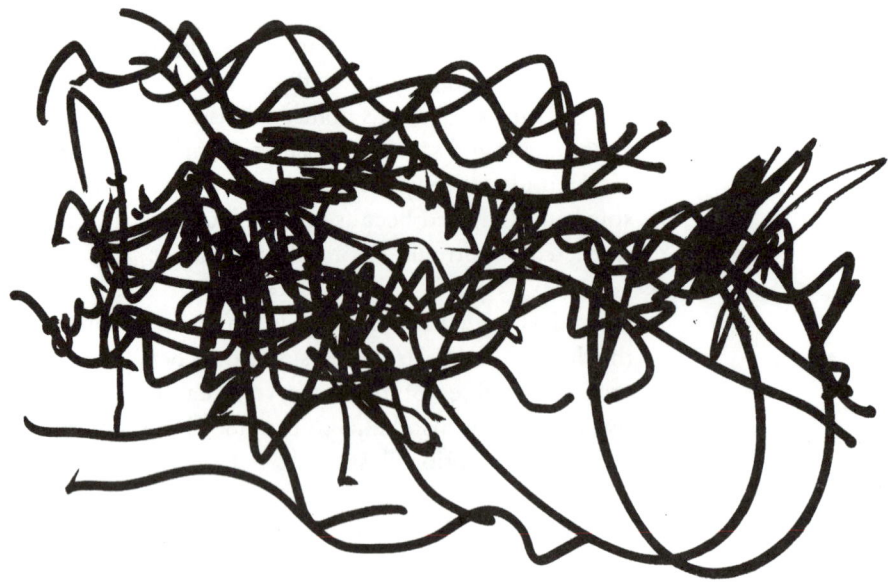

Clare, age 3, had the confidence to begin making marks as soon as she started in the nursery

develop a love of books and reading, and to connect children with a vast store of knowledge, information, fact and fantasy. Libraries also provide information about local preschool provision, services and events for young children.

FAMILY SUPPORT SERVICES

Parenting is a difficult, demanding role which most of us learn on the job, usually through trial and error, often with more error than trial. Taking a child to a playgroup or drop-in centre can provide much-needed contact with others, and can lead to mutual support.

It is not unusual for families to require additional help from experts in the fields of community health, social services or education. This is particularly the case for children who have special needs, perhaps a hearing loss or a physical disability. They may require a wide range of services to help them achieve their full potential, and you should not hesitate to ask for these for your child if you need them.

For some children, their special needs will be diagnosed at birth and parents will be given access to the relevant services. For example, Nathan was born with cerebral palsy and received a wide variety of support at different stages in his development. This included a specialist paediatrician, the community health team, a speech therapist, a physiotherapist and, by the time he was three, the special educational needs advisory team. All of these experts worked in collaboration with Nathan's parents and his nursery teacher to provide a coherent, shared approach to his development. It was much more effective than one person working alone, or several adults all doing unrelated things.

Children with special needs should not be prevented from having access to preschool settings, but again there are wide variations in what is available locally. The emphasis now is on integrating children into mainstream forms of provision, but special schools are still available. These may be suitable for some children as they offer a wide range of specialist facilities and family support services, including residential and respite care.

For some children, their special needs may only become apparent during infancy, for example, hearing difficulties or a delay in some aspect of physical or mental development. Seeking help and support is essential, as often problems which are diagnosed at an early stage can be remedied or at least alleviated. Nowadays the emphasis is very much on working in collaboration with the family, frequently in the home. For example, many local authorities run the *Portage scheme*, which can be used both in the home and in different preschool settings. The scheme involves providing an individually tailored programme to support children's learning and development, based on shared expertise, and trained Portage specialists work in partnership with parents and caregivers.

For many years some people working in education regarded parents as rude intruders, best kept in a cupboard. It is recognized increasingly that, if you are a parent, you actually have expert knowledge about your own child which is of great value to professionals. However, parenting does not always come easily, and some parents may require help with developing the skills to build positive relationships with their children. Parentcraft classes are run in a variety of settings including family and combined centres, nursery schools, the local health centre or in local colleges. There is no stigma attached to asking for help in becoming a good parent. After all, experts have to undergo long and rigorous periods of professional development to obtain their qualifications. In contrast, parents undertake one of the most difficult and challenging roles of adult life with little or no preparation.

WHERE CAN YOU GET INFORMATION?

The Children Act (1989) requires local authorities to undertake a review of provision and services every three years. This provides a comprehensive overview of what is available and where. The information is made available in local libraries, community or health centres. It can also be obtained by ringing the education department of the local council.

In addition local playgroups, private schools and nurseries often advertise in the local press. Noticeboards in supermarkets, health centres, libraries, shop windows, doctors' surgeries and churches provide information about playcentres, drop-in centres and parent/toddler groups. Family and combined centres provide information about other services and can help parents to use them according to their needs. Often the local grapevine or recommendations from other parents can be a valuable starting point.

NURSERY EDUCATION VOUCHERS

In 1996 the Department for Education and Employment began experiments with a new scheme for helping parents of four-year-old-children to meet the cost of a place in public, private and voluntary sector provision. The intention was to provide a full year of good quality education for every four-year-old-child. The scheme was launched in four areas, and parents received vouchers for every term a child was four years old, which could be worth up to £1100 per year. They were provided with a list of schools, playgroups and day nurseries in their local area which could accept the vouchers.

How the voucher could be used differed according to which type of provision was chosen or was available. In state nursery and primary schools the voucher covered a part-time place, or a full-time place if that was offered. It was also possible to use the voucher in local authority day nurseries. In private nurseries and playgroups the voucher covered fees up to £1100 a year, with parents making up the rest.

Many parents did not realize that the vouchers were also needed even if their four year olds attended state-funded primary and nursery schools, including those in the reception class of an infant school. The school needed them to claim back the money it was costing. However, parents were not able to use their voucher to obtain a part-time place in a private nursery school or playgroup, and then get a free state-funded place as well.

How far the voucher scheme will spread, and how it might change over the coming years, is not yet clear. However, nurseries and other preschool settings that want to join the voucher scheme have to:

- publish information on their staff (including their qualifications), premises and equipment;
- agree to work towards a set of goals for children's learning;
- be inspected during the first year after joining the scheme to make sure they are meeting the standards set.

Inspections of nurseries are carried out by the same body that inspects schools, the Office for Standards in Education (OFSTED), against established criteria in the following areas:

- the curriculum offered;
- the quality of learning;
- the quality of teaching;
- behaviour and discipline;
- assessment, recording and reporting on children's learning and development;
- resources, staffing and accommodation.

Linked to the voucher scheme is a requirement to prove that preschools can achieve certain goals for learning by the time children are five, which is the compulsory age for starting school. These goals are known as the *Desirable Learning Outcomes*. We return to this topic in greater depth on page 15.

MAKING YOUR CHOICE

It is likely that many children will experience different caregivers and forms of provision in their first five years. Whatever provision is chosen, parents should ensure that it is suitable for their child and provides a good balance between care and education. For example some private nurseries, particularly in the independent schools sector, tend to emphasize formal activities which concentrate on literacy and numeracy. Sitting very young children down for long periods of time with worksheets, or lots of teacher-directed activities, is regarded as poor educational practice by many teachers. Yet some parents say they want the 'get them in and get them on' approach from an early age. Others feel that formal methods which imitate later schooling are not in the best interests of young children and may even hinder their development as confident learners.

In the public sector it is now widely recognized that all forms of provision should provide both *care* and *education* to support children's learning and development. The two are not mutually exclusive. There is a wealth of research to show that good quality education in the first five years of a child's life has a positive influence which lasts through schooling and into adulthood. Parents, caregivers and teachers have a shared responsibility to ensure that children's formative experiences are of high quality, are well matched to their needs and interests, and promote their development as individuals in their own right.

Don't over emphasise formal activities

It has to be said that the quality of provision for young children is variable. Much of it is good, some is satisfactory (though not exciting) and some is simply poor. Inspection should help to raise standards and ensure that children experience an appropriate curriculum. If you are looking for a place for your child you have to probe beneath the surface to make sure you get the best quality available for your child.

This means you have to know what to look for, in both home-based and centre-based provision. The health, safety and welfare of children are fundamental requirements. In addition there are certain features which contribute to the overall quality of experience for children. Here are a few points to focus on. They are not given in any order of priority and some will apply more to centre-based than to home-based provision.

OTHER SIGNIFICANT ADULTS

Look closely at the people who will be looking after your child. Who are they? What will they do? Are they fit to work with children? The quality of relationships between parents, children, caregivers and teachers can have a significant influence on the quality of experience, so people are an important factor. The staff should be warm and responsive, able to communicate well with parents and able to talk and play with children.

The Children Act (1989) provides a comprehensive definition of 'a fit person' to work with young children which includes:

- previous experience of looking after or working with children;
- qualifications and/or training in a relevant field;
- the ability to provide warm and consistent care;
- knowledge of equal opportunities;
- commitment to treat all children as individuals and with equal concern;
- physical health;
- mental stability, integrity and flexibility.

The local health, education and social services departments are empowered to ensure that staff have no known convictions in criminal cases involving abuse to children or in other relevant cases.

Parents will want to satisfy themselves that they are leaving their children in the hands of caring, competent people with a commitment to their work and a genuine liking for young children. There are a variety of qualifications for childcare and education from the age of sixteen upwards. It may be the case that some assistants in daycare settings (in both the public and private sectors) will have no formal training, but they should be under the supervision of those who have, and provision should be made for staff development.

Other adults may hold a range of qualifications in the fields of social work, health or education. For example, all teachers in primary schools have to obtain qualified teacher status by following a four-year degree which specializes in education, or a one-year Postgraduate Certificate in Education course if they already have a degree. Increasingly there are multidisciplinary courses which reflect the fact that the expertise required of professionals who work with young children is highly specialized but quite diverse.

Opportunities for staff to attend courses and keep up to date should ensure that they know all about legal requirements and government initiatives, and that they are knowledgeable about the most effective ways of providing care and education for young children.

Some nurseries operate a '*key worker*' system. This means that one or possibly two particular adults are assigned to a child. They are the people responsible for liaison with parents and caregivers. This system maintains continuity and stability, especially for young babies, so that they learn to attach themselves to another significant person, rather than having to adapt to a constant stream of different people. Often the key workers will keep responsibility for the same group of children as they progress right through the nursery. Many nurseries try hard to make their provision warm and responsive, as much like home as possible, so that the children do not feel 'institutionalized'.

THE LEARNING ENVIRONMENT

They may not sit in rows copying off the blackboard, but much valuable learning is available for children. Both the indoor and outdoor environment are important for their learning and general development. Look for the following.

Indoors

The environment should be bright and welcoming to both parents and children. Where space is available there may be an entrance hall where parents can come with their children and talk to staff at the beginning or end of the day. It is common practice to provide a notice-board with photographs of who's who, information about trips, special events and the curriculum, and requests for help or resources.

The variety of resources will vary according to the setting chosen and the age group of the children. Where children are likely to be in the same nursery for some time provision should be tailored for the different age groups. For example, Duplo building bricks are suitable up to the age of three or four, but children need the opportunity to progress to Lego to learn new skills and extend their capabilities.

Typical provision for young children tends to include sand and water trays, large and small building blocks, small world play such as Mobilo, Playmobil and Lego, an area for role play and dressing up, a book corner, space for table top games and puzzles, and an area for creativity. Often playgroups are not very well resourced with the larger, more expensive items, but will provide a range of other activities. Where space is limited the staff may rotate the resources to provide variety and balance.

The learning environment should be well organized, with resources easily accessible to the children. Containers, drawers and cupboards should be labelled with a picture and writing to help children identify the contents and help them make choices independently. This system also encourages children to put things away at the end of the session!

Where display space is available this should reflect mainly the children's and not the adults' work. If adults use templates for the children's 'art', or draw outlines for them to fill in with tissue paper, this undervalues the children's own creative processes and their abilities to represent their thinking and experience in different ways. It might look nice to adults, but it doesn't have much relevance for the children if they have had little involvement. It is valuable to have a variety of displays of, for example, natural materials, machinery or artefacts associated with different religious festivals, to which children and their families can contribute. This encourages home–school links and can ensure that different lifestyles and cultures are represented.

Outdoors

Children should, ideally, have space to run around and play with bikes and other wheeled toys. This provides opportunities for them to enjoy fresh air and to develop coordination of their large muscles through running, skipping, pushing, pulling, pedalling. They can also play more boisterous chasing or adventure games which are difficult to accommodate indoors. You will often find your children pleasantly tired if they have had an opportunity for good physical activity, which can be preferable to their having been penned up all day and dying to rampage around when they get home.

An ideal setting might include hard paving and grassed areas, space for growing plants, shaded areas for hot weather and space for children to sit as well as run around. Many purpose-built nursery schools have a covered verandah, so that the children can enjoy outdoor play even in cold, wet or hot weather.

Liam loved drawing and included many complex details in his pictures. He also enjoyed writing letters and numerals, and learned to write his name correctly before starting school.

THE CURRICULUM

It may seem strange to use the word 'curriculum' in relation to children under five. Could this mean life is like it is in secondary schools, with timetables, exams and subject-specialist teachers? Not at all. The word 'curriculum' simply means 'a programme of learning', and that is exactly what young children have, whether it is the informal curriculum of home, or the planned experiences and activities in a preschool setting.

Even babies can have a curriculum, but it is a very informal one. For example, changing a nappy can be seen on the one hand as an arduous task, to be done in the quickest possible time. On the other hand it can provide valuable opportunities for interaction between a child and the parents or caregiver. Babies respond to positive touch, voice and eye contact, all of which form part of the bonding process. These interactions also help children relate to and engage with other people.

All nurseries and playgroups are required by law to provide a balance of care and education. So people who look after children can all be seen as educators, and they should have a clear view of the range of activities and experiences which are appropriate for young children at different ages, and the learning opportunities these present. Ideally there should be a balance between child-initiated and adult-directed activities. Many nurseries also try to provide routines and experiences which mirror children's home lives, such as trips to the shops, park or places of interest.

For example, one nursery took the children for a teddy bears' picnic. The children planned, bought and made the food, designed paper napkins, decided where they wanted to go and, of course, brought along their own favourite toy. Involving children in activities helps them to make choices and decisions, to take responsibility and to feel as if they have a valuable contribution to make. If all the decisions are made by adults this is unlikely to produce confident learners.

The year before children begin compulsory schooling at the age of five is particularly important in enabling them to become confident learners and make the transition to being a school pupil. In 1996 the School Curriculum and Assessment Authority (SCAA) recommended learning goals for four-year-old-children based on *Desirable Learning Outcomes*. These outcomes are linked to the nursery voucher scheme and places which want to register for the scheme have to prove that they are able to achieve them through the curriculum offered.

These Desirable Learning Outcomes are based on six areas of learning:

- personal and social development;
- language and literacy;
- mathematics;
- knowledge and understanding of the world;
- physical development;
- creative development.

Each area of learning is defined by a set of skills, knowledge and competences which children are expected to have attained by the age of five. Once children start school at the age of five they will begin the first Key Stage (lasting from age five up to age seven) of an eleven-year National Curriculum. These outcomes have been specially designed to overlap with the very first steps of the National Curriculum to promote continuity of learning and experience as children make the transition to infant school. More information about this first stage of school is contained in the *Guide to Key Stage 1* in this series.

COPING WITH THE CHANGE

The day eventually comes when children leave their parents, even if only for a short time. For some children this is at the age of five, when they start school, but for the thousands who attend preschools or go to caregivers it is earlier.

Leaving a child in the care of another adult can be a traumatic experience. For a start most of us are convinced that we alone can give our child what he or she needs. It can be quite threatening to discover that they quite like the company of other adults. Most of us recoil when our child comes out with, 'Well, Mrs Preston says...' Oh, does she really? And just who is this smarty pants Mrs Preston, who is now being quoted admiringly by our child as the world's leading authority on everything that we used to be the local expert on?

Children too may be apprehensive about leaving their parents for a short while the first time it happens. This difficult moment can be managed in different ways according to the age of the child. Places which strive to provide a high quality of care and education have the best interests of children at heart and will be aware of parents' anxieties at leaving their children, whether this is for a part-time session in a nursery class or for full-time day care. They are well used to the situation and they will provide you with reassurance and information about your child's progress.

Introducing a baby to a new caregiver or a new place should be a gradual process during which a parent is present. If possible withdraw for a short while and gradually leave the child for longer periods of time, so it gets used to the idea that Mum or Dad will reappear. When you are tiny, it is not easy to understand that Mum and Dad still exist when they are not with you. It is only when they have reappeared a few times that you begin to realize they have not fallen off the planet.

Similarly for older children, separations should be gradual. On his first day in a nursery class, Wayne arrived at nine o'clock. One hour later he put on his coat, announced he had had enough, and said he was going home. It took a lot of persuasion to encourage him to stay! Life is often made easier if it is explained to a child what will be happening. However, it is difficult for a three year old to understand that Mum or Dad will be back at three o'clock when it is only nine o'clock, and they have no idea what will be going on in between, or what 'six hours' or 'three o'clock' actually mean.

Many nurseries now have a shared record-keeping system which allows parents, educators and caregivers to contribute comments and observations, photographs and examples of work. This can also provide an interesting record of development and achievement which children can contribute to as they get older. It also helps to inform parents about educational goals and the purpose of activities.

STARTING SCHOOL

It is important to give positive messages about any setting outside the home, especially when starting school. One mother, visibly frustrated, dragged her son across the threshold of a reception class with the words 'Here you are Miss, sort him out will you, I can't do a thing with him.' Hardly a positive start to school for the child, parent or teacher, and one to be avoided. Equally bad is threatening children with schools or teachers – 'They'll soon sort you out, my lad/lass when you start school.' It makes school sound like some kind of medieval torture chamber. Much better that parents give their children a head start by making sure they have the following skills and attitudes:

- self-confidence and a positive sense of self;
- positive attitudes towards learning, having a go, trying out new ideas and experiences;
- being able to interact with children and other adults;
- self-help skills, such as looking after property, hanging up coats, getting dressed and undressed, putting on shoes, fastening buttons;
- using a toilet correctly and washing hands afterwards.

Most schools now have strategies for introducing children to school. These include home visits, children attending story sessions in the term before they start, half-day sessions for the first few weeks to get children used to new routines and experiences, or reception class teachers may visit local playgroups and nurseries so that their faces are familiar.

Using a toilet correctly

Parents and other adults can and do make a tremendous difference in the first five years of a child's life and all have a responsibility to provide children with a good start. It is helpful to have some understanding of early learning and development. If you understand how children's language, feelings and intelligence grow during these early years then you can work in harmony with the playgroup or nursery and this can give vital support. So we shall now look at some of the information that it is helpful for parents to have.

EARLY LEARNING AND DEVELOPMENT

Being a good parent and educator does not happen overnight, and it certainly isn't a natural, in-built process which slides smoothly into gear the moment your child is born. It takes time, energy, patience, dedication, stamina, tolerance, understanding and knowledge. All children are individuals who grow, learn and develop in their own ways and at their own pace. There are broad similarities in the patterns of children's development, but wide differences in the pace. For example, one child may learn to walk by nine months, another by two years. Often children do not conform to the neat averages and patterns set out in books on child development, and it is usually unhelpful to believe that there is a mythical 'ideal parent' or way of parenting, or indeed an 'ideal child'.

When children are born they have natural tendencies towards being *active*, *curious* and *sociable*. These are the foundations of learning. Because of their inexperience children need a lot of help along the way, so that they make the most of this great appetite for learning. Parents and nursery staff can easily capitalize on their curiosity, for example.

Children are naturally active because they have an inner drive to make sense of the world in which they live, and their place in it. Gradually they learn to control their bodies, actions and interactions with other people. They need lots of practice and repetition to acquire a range of skills which gradually enable them to become more independent. Their activity needs to be channelled into a wide range of experiences with different opportunities for learning.

Children are naturally curious as they strive to discover and explore their environment and everything in it. To achieve a sense of mastery they need to find out what things do, what can be done with them, what they need help with and what they can do alone. Children should be encouraged to try things out, both on their own and with help, in a safe environment, so that they learn to persevere, solve problems and experience that 'I *can* do this' feeling. As well as achieving a sense of mastery children need to develop a belief in their capabilities as learners. *Positive attitudes* towards learning, finding out and having a go are important qualities for later success in school.

Most children are naturally sociable and a great deal of learning takes place in social situations with parents, family members, caregivers and friends. From the moment of birth babies tune into their environment and respond to other people. This level of responsiveness and attachment is part of the bonding process between parents and children, but it is also the foundation of the teaching and learning relationship. This relationship begins at birth and involves many complex processes and interactions. Sometimes parents are unaware of the amount of teaching they are doing as they often regard it as part of their natural, spontaneous ways of simply being with a child. Whenever you talk with and listen to a child, for example, you are helping him or her acquire that vital and miraculous human tool – *language*.

Through interacting with other people in many different situations children gradually learn how to become social and sociable. They learn about acceptable behaviour, rules and routines, how to make relationships and how to take their place in a complex and demanding world. In order to do this they have to process and understand a great deal of information, acquire knowledge and become aware of themselves as individuals as well as members of a family and society. So how does all this come about in such a short time?

We have seen that children are active, curious and sociable, that they are 'pretuned' for learning and are responsive to people and their environment. Therefore they need certain conditions to help them to learn and develop, such as:

- warm, responsive relationships with parents, family members, caregivers and teachers;
- a stimulating environment which is safe but encourages exploration, finding out and a certain amount of risk taking;
- varied resources (toys, games, materials, objects) which stimulate different skills and help children to acquire knowledge;
- a wide variety of experiences and activities, some presented by an adult and some initiated by the child;
- a great deal of support, praise and encouragement to help them achieve a positive sense of themselves as individuals.

LANGUAGE AND EXPERIENCE

Young children are eager, competent learners. They learn by direct experience and at the heart of this is the development of their language. Experience is acquired through all five senses – sight, sound, touch, taste and smell. Watch how babies stare at things, handle them, put them into their mouths. They are using their senses to learn about the world around them. Gradually children get to know what things are and what can be done with them. They learn to control their actions and to understand the possibilities that increasing control brings, as the following example shows.

By the age of eight months Elizabeth could stand against a sofa. One of her favourite games was putting different toys on a small tin tray with a rim. At first she concentrated on hand and eye coordination to pick up the toys and place them on the tray. She noticed that the toys made different sounds against the tray, so she started to bang or throw them on to it, to amplify the sound. Sometimes she banged them against the sofa first to compare the effects of her actions on different surfaces.

One day she leaned on the tray and saw that it tipped over and everything fell off. This became a game, and she would fill the tray then deliberately tip it over, sometimes banging herself on the forehead in the process. Gradually she learned to stand aside to tip the tray. Then she learned that if she hit the rim the toys would fly out on to the sofa and carpet. The game then reached a different stage. She experimented with hitting the tray to see how far everything could be scattered. Sometimes she played this game alone, but it was usually more fun with adults, especially if they helped pick up all the toys!

Elizabeth was learning to control her actions, and the objects, materials and people in her environment. This simple activity encouraged sensory exploration, hand and eye coordination, strengthened her leg and back muscles, developed her ability to use her hands and fingers (fine motor control) and gave her hours of fun. But most importantly it showed that she was an active thinker and an energetic learner. Such activities might seem quite trivial to adults, especially when they involve a lot of repetition, but to young children they are deeply meaningful. The challenge for parents, and for other adults who come into contact with children, is to recognize these patterns of action, learning and behaviour and to try and support children in their endeavours to make sense of the world and to build a store of knowledge and information.

Just as parents nourish children's growing bodies with food, they need to nourish their developing minds. What might seem easy to an adult is immensely complex to a young child – putting one brick on top of another, trying to figure out why some things float in the bath and other things sink, how to pedal a bike. But children cannot learn everything through exploration and discovery and an important role for parents is using language to support children's learning and development.

Because young children are active, curious and sociable it is thought that they are 'pretuned' to respond to language from babyhood. Even when alone, babies experiment with using their voices and learn quickly what gains immediate attention. Parents naturally talk to babies as part of their caregiving and bonding. 'Dat two mouses,' says Ian, pointing to a picture in a book. 'Oh yes,' says his mother, 'I can see two mice in that picture.' 'Ah ha!' thinks little Ian, 'so the word "mouse" has an irregular plural, then.' Except that he doesn't think in those terms. He simply learns, by listening to others and trying it out for himself, how language works.

Babies experimenting with their voices

We all have our own ways of bringing up our children, but there are some common approaches which can benefit children's learning and development and help them in school and in later life. They include:

- Show interest in children. This is one of the most fundamental ways in which a child will learn that he or she is valued and has a place in the world.

- Respond to children from the earliest cooings and babblings to the searching questions of a curious four year old. Listening and responding to a child gives the message that they have things which are important to say, and are worth listening to. This builds self-confidence and self-esteem.

- Give support, but don't take over. It is valuable to demonstrate or talk through a new skill, as long as the child can have a go without worrying about getting it wrong.

- Help children to experience success and cope with mistakes. Even experienced learners get things wrong sometimes, but for children this can cause frustration and temper tantrums. Seeing mistakes as an opportunity to learn is a positive way of dealing with them.

- Concentrate on what a child is saying and doing – take this seriously and give it full attention. If you always iron or watch television when they try to talk to you this gives negative messages to a child.

- Be responsive to a child's existing level of skill and knowledge and use this as the foundation for new learning.

- Talk about what a child has done. This can be useful for helping him or her to remember newly learned skills and knowledge, develop language and communication skills, and to be valued.

- Give praise and positive reinforcement. If children are told that they are stupid and useless this is what they will believe about themselves and, more worryingly, will act accordingly. If they are given positive messages about themselves as people and as learners then they will be better able to take their place in the world with confidence.

- Make time for them to play alone, with other children, parents and other adults.

LEARNING THROUGH PLAY

Young children and young animals love to play and spend a great deal of time doing it. Yet we do not fully understand why play occurs and what purposes it serves. Most children find that play is enjoyable, fun, interesting and absorbing. It provides lots of opportunities for children to make choices, explore, discover, take control, practise skills, learn new skills and acquire knowledge about themselves, objects, materials and the environment. So play is not just a trivial, babyish activity which keeps children occupied until they are old enough for the more serious business of work. In terms of children's learning and development all types of play provide serious and meaningful experiences, which is why good quality preschool settings incorporate play into their curriculum.

Play provides ideal opportunities for children to be curious, active and sociable. They learn how to play in collaboration with other children and adults. Probably one of the first games they learn to play is 'peek-a-boo', where an adult moves in and out of a child's view and pretends to be hiding, often behind a piece of material. Because this is seen as playing, parents might not fully realize how much valuable learning is going on. In just this one simple game, played over a period of time, a child will learn:

- to focus on the player;
- to follow the player with her eyes;
- to take turns;
- that the player does not disappear, but is hiding;
- that the player will reappear;
- that interacting with an adult can be fun and pleasurable;
- that her actions cause a response in the player;
- that she can take some control over the actions;
- that she can eventually play this game with another adult, child or toy.

The role of adults in children's play is quite complex. On the one hand, parents who are good players can offer a model of some of the skills needed for the children to become good players. For example, in learning how to play board games, children have first to learn and then to observe the rules, take turns and understand the purpose and sequence of the game. These are complex skills which cannot just be 'discovered'. They actually have to be learned with the support of a 'more knowledgeable' adult or child.

On the other hand, children themselves are perfectly capable of playing alone or in a group. Watch them when they are at play. From around the age of three they can make up long sequences of imaginative play, where they create their own rules and act out different roles. For imaginative play to be successful children have to know how to cooperate, take turns, communicate their ideas, listen to other children's ideas and share toys and props. So there is a great deal of learning going on during play.

Sometimes it is useful for adults to engage in imaginative play to help children to learn some of these skills as well as to just enjoy playing together. In these situations parents and caregivers can act as a role model but must be careful not to direct or take over the play. Playing on a child's terms and in response to requests or suggestions is an essential skill to learn, again because it values the child's ideas and actions.

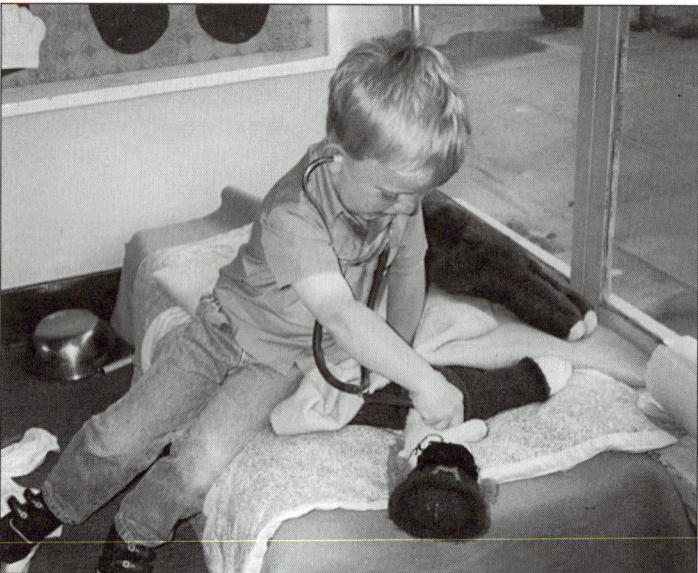

Combining knowledge, experience and imagination in play

What to play with

There is no shortage of toys and games to buy for young children, from baby's first rattle to sophisticated computer games. Parents will make their choices according to their own and their children's preferences. For example, some prefer not to buy toy guns and swords because they believe it leads to aggressive behaviour, or encourages children to think that they can only feel powerful if they have a weapon in their hands. Parents have a right to exercise such choices on behalf of their children but, as one mother found, as soon as her son went to nursery he engaged in exactly the sort of play she had actively discouraged for the first four years of his life. This shows how the influence of friends and the media can start to become more significant as children get older.

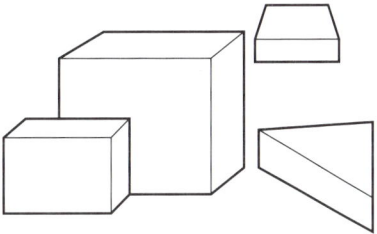

- Playing and learning
- Creating and solving problems
- Fitting shapes together
- Talking about size, shape and colour
- Noticing differences and similarities
- Practicing hand-eye co-ordination

- Having fun, concentrating and persevering
- Sharing and co-operating with children and adults
- Asking questions, taking control
- Designing and making
- Using creativity and investigating
- Exploring and investigating

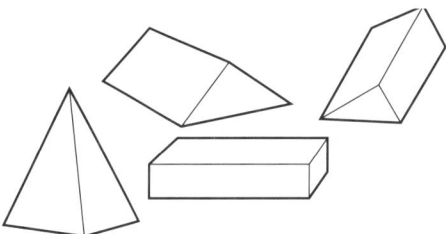

Learning through play – building bricks.

Young children need a wide variety of toys, games, activities, objects and resources to keep them busy and stimulate learning. But good quality play doesn't have to come with a high price tag. Many parents have had the experience of bringing home a large, expensive toy, only to find that their child was more interested in playing with the cardboard box! The basic rule is that anything given to a child must be safe and, on this basis, everyday items around the home can be every bit as stimulating as commercially produced toys.

Remember that young children learn through their five senses and through exploration, particularly in early infancy. It follows that they need a variety of materials and resources to stimulate their understanding of texture, shape and size, and to compare and contrast. A popular idea in some nurseries is providing children with a 'treasure basket' which is a large, open container which allows access to a wide variety of resources. These can include cotton reels, lollipop sticks, string, different lengths and colours of ribbon, bottle tops, small plastic containers, corks, lengths of chain and pieces of wood. As children get older other things can be added, for example large marbles, buttons and beads, conkers, corrugated card and sandpaper.

Children should be allowed free, undirected time to explore their treasure basket, so that they can experience all the different objects. It is not unusual for children to sort them out on the basis of size, shape, colour and texture, or to make patterns – all of which are valuable mathematical skills. Parents and caregivers may join in sometimes, to introduce language or to draw attention to what a child has done. Like all interactions, this should be a positive experience for the child, with no pressure to perform in a certain way.

As children get older they expand their skills, knowledge and understanding in many different areas. Play continues to provide valuable experiences, especially as children start to play with ideas, roles and relationships. It is even possible, with appropriate experiences and activities, that children can 'play' their way into reading and writing, and learn a wide variety of skills and knowledge which help them in school.

BECOMING READERS, WRITERS AND MATHEMATICIANS

Parents are often concerned about how much 'teaching' of reading, writing and mathematics they should do at home, especially now that children are given tests in school at the age of seven, and increasingly at five, for their skills in these areas.

Many parents may believe that the complex processes of learning to read and write are best left to teachers when children begin school. They may think that they do not have the specialist skills and resources, or that reading is all about 'phonics', flash cards and specially graded schemes. In fact, the opposite is true, and one of the most important influences on their success is the amount of support they receive in the home. This does not mean that all parents should arm themselves with flashcards and a 'Fun with Phonics' manual. Learning to read and write is an exciting journey of discovery which opens up new areas of experience and meaning for children. Parents and caregivers have an important role to play in guiding children on this journey.

BECOMING A READER

Children are born into societies which depend on many different forms of communication. They are surrounded by print, signs and symbols in all kinds of places. For example, labels, logos and messages on clothing, toys and games; street signs, advertising hoardings, on the television and computer games and programmes. Learning what those signs and symbols mean is the first step on the journey to literacy. Although children may not be able to read the words parents can help them to learn to distinguish between words and pictures, and to understand that both convey meaning in different ways. You can 'read' or tell a story without any print by interpreting the pictures with children.

Sharing books with children serves many important purposes such as extending vocabulary, enriching the imagination and conveying knowledge and information. It is best to give quiet, dedicated time to this, without the distractions of television or radio, so that children can learn to enjoy the shared experience and benefit from the interactions. Sharing books helps to unlock the mysteries of reading, teaches children how to use books, to interpret the words and pictures and respond to the text. So some useful strategies are:

BECOMING READERS, WRITERS AND MATHEMATICS 25

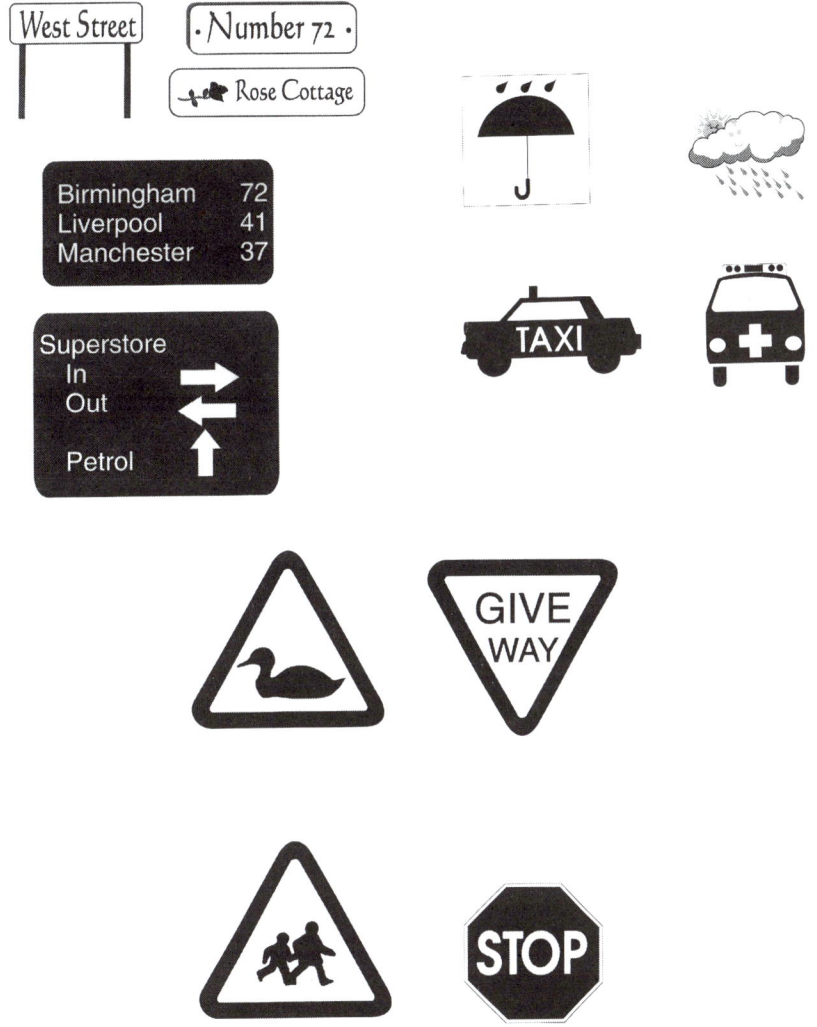

Children live in a print-rich environment. Noticing signs and symbols, and interpreting what they mean helps them to understand some of the purposes for reading and writing.

- Make time to share and enjoy books – stories, poetry, fact and fiction.
- Show a child how to handle a book – right way up and front to back.
- Explain the difference between words and pictures.
- Explain the direction in which print is read, according to the language used – in English this is left to right, in Chinese top to bottom, in Arabic right to left.
- Encourage a child to 'pretend' to read – often favourite stories, rhymes and poems are memorized and the child can believe that he is reading – a positive step on the journey.
- Encourage children to notice words and symbols around them – street signs, advertising hoardings, on television programmes and in computer games.
- Explain the different purposes for which adults need to read and demonstrate these to the children, for example newspapers, instructions, map reading, letters.

BECOMING A WRITER

Similarly with writing, children can make a lot of progress before they start school. Scribbling is the first step in making marks, which leads to understanding that those marks can convey meaning. So never criticize a child's early drawing, painting and mark making if it doesn't resemble anything recognizable. The important point is that it has meaning for the child and he should be able to talk about that to someone who is genuinely interested in his efforts. Again parents and caregivers can provide lots of support.

Playing and learning – becoming a reader and writer

- Have materials for children to make marks – painting, drawing, printing, with pens, pencils and crayons of different thickness. A bucket of water and brush is great for painting pictures and symbols outside. Children enjoy finger writing in different media such as wet sand or a mix of cornflour and water.

- Explain the different purposes for writing and let children imitate those. They love writing letters, notes, messages, prescriptions for toys that are 'poorly' or shopping lists, and adults should value their efforts and share their meanings.

- Display children's writing at home, for example on a message board, and encourage other family members to participate in sharing writing.

- Provide a model of correct symbols and writing. Often children like to copy or trace these, but this shouldn't be forced, as there is a difference between 'being a writer' and 'practising handwriting'. Children learn gradually to copy words, numerals and symbols by understanding that they have meaning and convey messages. Often they begin to incorporate these into their painting and drawing to show their understanding and practise the shapes.

BECOMING READERS, WRITERS AND MATHEMATICS 27

Michelle enjoyed writing letters and numerals and spent time at the writing table every day. She was interested in books and often took one home from the nursery to share with her Mum.

BECOMING A MATHEMATICIAN

Mathematics is another area which is of concern to parents, particularly if they were not competent in this subject themselves. But it is amazing how much children learn about mathematics, again through everyday experiences, interactions and play. Mathematics is not just about doing hard sums. It involves noticing similarities and differences; recognizing patterns, shapes, sizes, colours; comparing, sorting, matching; and counting, ordering and sequencing. In playing with bricks, children will notice different shapes and sizes, how they fit together, how many bricks they use to build a tower, who has got the most bricks, and how to get more! Parents can talk and play with their children to introduce new language, skills and concepts and to encourage problem-solving skills.

Similarly everyday activities, such as 'baking', provide valuable opportunities to talk about weighing and measuring, filling containers, timing a recipe, counting the number of biscuits made or sharing out a cake. Going shopping involves buying and selling, handling money, recognizing the value of coins, writing cheques, deciding what can be afforded. All these experiences can be explained to children so that they start to understand how mathematics is used in everyday life. It is amazing how much real-world knowledge they pick up by being with parents and educators who communicate with them, respond to and stimulate interest, and take the time to explain, describe, demonstrate and allow the children to have a go themselves.

These are the sorts of valuable learning experiences which good quality preschool settings will encourage through play and teacher-directed activities. If children act as readers, writers and mathematicians, they will become confident at 'having a go', rather than being wary of making mistakes. They will learn some of the language needed to help them to learn new skills and competences as they forge ahead in their learning and development.

The first five years of a child's life are a period of such rapid learning and development that all those who share in the process of care and education have a responsibility to make their experiences as good as possible. Young children have enormous potential. In spite of all the agonies of parenting they are a source of endless fascination and joy. They are people in their own right, and how they are treated in childhood has a lasting influence throughout their lives.

Young children are our newest citizens, all our future. They should take their place in the world with confidence and belief in themselves and what they can do.

Kirsty combined drawing, writing, shapes and symbols. She was beginning to copy words and concentrate hard on what she was doing.

Addresses

British Association for Early Childhood Education
111 City View House
463 Bethnal Green Road
London E2 9QY

British Dyslexia Association
98 London Road
Reading
RG1 5AU

Campaign for State Education (CASE)
158 Durham Road
London
SW20 0DG

Curriculum and Assessment Authority for Wales (ACAC)
Castle Buildings
Womanby Street
Cardiff
CF1 9SX

Department for Education and Employment
Sanctuary Buildings
Great Smith Street
London
SW1P 3BT

Her Majesty's Stationery Office (HMSO)
Publications Centre
51 Nine Elms Lane
London
SW8 5DR

Independent Schools Information Service (ISIS)
56 Buckingham Gate
London
SW1E 6AG

National Association for Gifted Children
Park Campus
Boughton Green Road
Northampton
NN2 7AL

ADDRESSES

National Association of Governors and Managers
21 Bennetts Hill
Birmingham
B2 5QP

National Campaign for Nursery Education
BCM Box 6216
London WC1N 3XX

National Children's Bureau
Early Childhood Unit
8 Wakley Street
London NW1 3AL

National Children's Play and Recreation Unit
359-361 Euston Road
London NW1 3AL

National Confederation of Parent-Teacher Associations
2 Ebbsfleet Industrial Estate
Stonebridge Road
Gravesend
Kent
DA11 9DZ

National Council for Voluntary Organisations
Regents Wharf
8 All Saints Street
London N1 9RL

National Early Years Network
77 Holloway Road
London NW7 8JZ

Office for Standards in Education (OFSTED)
Alexandra House
33 Kingsway
London
WC1B 6SE

Preschool Learning Alliance
69 King's Cross Road
London WC 1X 9LL

School Curriculum and Assessment Authority
Newcombe House
45 Notting Hill Gate
London
W11 3JB

Welsh Office Education Department
Cathays Park
Cardiff
CF1 3NQ